Sammel- und Bestimmungsbuch für Retro-Spiele

AF211499

Nintendo NES (c)
Nintendo SNES (c)
Nintendo 64 (c)

(c) 2016 - Sammelland-Verlag BadVilbel

Michael Graf
Friedbergerstr. 98
61118 Bad Vilbel
Tel: 0179/1473259
e-Mail: ep-verlagbadvilbel@web.de

Vorwort

Ein Bestimmungsbuch muss nicht teuer sein, um alle Bedürfnisse zu befriedigen. Der RETROgamer Katalog beinhaltet die Spiele der drei wichtigsten Nintendo-Konsolen.

Nintendo Entertainment System (c)
Super Nintendo Entertainment System (c)
Nintendo 64 (c)

Mit der Möglichkeit Spiele der eigenen Sammlung anzukreuzen.

Was enthält der Katalog?

Mit diesem Buch wird gearbeitet!

Alle Spiele sortiert nach Konsole und innerhalb der Kategorie nach dem Alphabeth. Enthalten sind PAL und NTSC Spiele. Nicht enthalten sind asiatische Games.

Die Sammlung kann über simples ankreuzen verwaltet werden. Dies ermöglicht einen ständigen Überblick über den Zustand der einzelnen Spiele.

Dies ist kein Sammlerkatalog im Sinne der Wertbestimmung. Dieses Buch dient der Verwaltung der eigenen Sammlung. Man kann darin festhalten, welche Spiele in welchem Zustand in der Sammlung sind. Dafür ist auf jeder Seite diese Zeile angedruckt.

Modul	Name	Inlay	OVP

Man kann darunter ankreuzen, ob man das Modul, das Inlay und die Verpackung in der Sammlung hat. Es sollte immer dabei sein, wenn man seine Sammlung vergrößtert.

NES Nintendo Entertainment System (c)

Technische Daten: 8 Bit Videospielkonsole
Auflösung: 256 x 240 Pixel
RAM: 2 KB
CPU: 1,77 MHz
Speichermedium: Modul (6 Mbit)
Verkaufszeitraum Europa: 1983 bis 1995

Verkaufte Einheiten: 61,8 Millionen weltweit

Zubehör:
- Fitnessmatte (Power Pad)
- NES Advantag - Joyboard
- NES Four Score - Adapter um bis zu 4 Controller anzuschließen
- Zapper Lightgun - Laserpistole

Modul	Name	Inlay	OVP
	1942 Capcom 1986		
	1943 Capcom 1988		
	10 Yard Fight Nintendo 1985		
	2 in 1 Super Mario Bros. / Duck Hunt Nintendo 1988		
	2 in 1 Super Bike / V Ball World Cup Soccer Nintendo 1990		
	3-D Worldrunner Acclaim 1987		
	3 in 1 Super Mario Bros / Duck Hunt / Wordl Class Track Meet Nintendo 1990		
	720 Degrees Mindscape 1989		
	8 Eyes Taxan 1990		
	A Nightmare on Elm Street LJN 1990		
	Abadox Milton Bradley 1990		
	Addams Family Ocean 1992		
	Addams Family - Pugsley´s Scavenger Hunt Ocean 1993		
	Advanced Dungeon & Dragons Dragonstrike FCI 1992		
	Advanced Dungeon & Dragons Heroes of the Lance FCI 1991		
	Advanced Dungeon & Dragons Hillsfar FCI 1993		

NES 03

Modul	Name	Inlay	OVP
	Advanced Dungeon & Dragons Poll of Radiance FCI 1992		
	Adventure Island Hudson Soft 1988		
	Adventure Island II Hudson Soft 1991		
	Adventure Island II Hudson Soft 1992		
	Adventures in the Magic Kindom Capcom 1990		
	Adventures of Bayou Billy Konami 1989		
	Adventures of Dino Riki Hudson Soft 1989		
	Adventures ofGilligan´s Island Bandai 1990		
	Adventures of Lolo Hal America 1989		
	Adventures of Lolo II Hal America 1990		
	Adventures of Lolo III Hal America 1991		
	Adventures of Rad Gravitiy Activision 1990		
	Adventures of Rocky & Bullwinkle and Friends THQ 1992		
	Adventures of Tom Sawyer Seta 1989		
	Air Fortress Hal America 1989		
	Airwolf Acclaim 1989		
	Al Unser Jr´s Turbo Racing Data East 1990		

Modul	Name	Inlay	OVP
	Alfred Chicken Mindscape 1994		
	Alien 3 LJN 1993		
	All Pro Basketball Cic Tokai 1989		
	Alpha Mission SNK 1987		
	Amagon American Sammy 1989		
	American Gladiators Gametek 1991		
	Anticipation Nintendo 1988		
	Arch Rivals - A Basket Brawl Acclaim 1990		
	Archon Activision 1989		
	Arkanoid Tatto Software 1987		
	Arkista´s Ring American Sammy 1990		
	Astyanax Jaleco 1990		
	Athema SNK 1987		
	Athletic World Bandai 1987		
	Attack of the Killer Tomatos THQ 1992		
	Back to Future LJN 1989		
	Back to Future II LJN 1990		
	Bad Dudes Data East 1990		

Modul	Name	Inlay	OVP
	Bad News Basketball Tecmo 1990		
	Bad News Brawler Mattell 1989		
	Balloon Fight Nintendo 1986		
	Bandai Golf Challenge Pebble Beach Bandai 1989		
	Bandit Kings of Ancient China Koei 1990		
	Barbie Hi-Tech 1991		
	Bard´s Tale FCI 1991		
	Barkers Bill´s Trick Shooting Nintendo 1990		
	Base Wars - Cyber Stadium Series Ultra Soft 1991		
	Baseball Nintendo 1985		
	Baseball Simulator 1000 Culture Brain 1990		
	Baseball Stars SNK 1989		
	Baseball Stars II Romstar 1992		
	Bases Loaded Jaleco 1988		
	Bases Loaded - Secon Season Jaleco 1990		
	Bases Loaded III Jaleco 1991		
	Bases Loaded IV Jaleco 1993		
	Batman Sunsoft 1990		

Modul	Name	Inlay	OVP
	Batman Return of the Joker Sunsoft 1991		
	Batman Returns Konami 1993		
	Batlle Chess Data East 1990		
	Battle of the Olympus Broderbund 1989		
	Battle Tank Absolute 1990		
	Battleship Mindscape 1993		
	Battletoads Tradewest 1991		
	Battletoads & Double Dragon The Ultimate Team Tradewest 1993		
	Beetlejuice LJN 1991		
	Best of the best - Championchip Karate Electro Brain 1992		
	Bigfoot Acclaim 1990		
	Bill & Ted's Excellent Video Game Adventure LJN 1991		
	Bill Elliot's Nascar Challange Konami 1991		
	Bionic Commando Capcom 1988		
	Black Bass Hot-B 1989		
	Blades of Steel Konami 1988		
	Blaster Master Sunsoft 1988		

Modul	Name	Inlay	OVP
	Blue Martin Hot-B 1992		
	Blues Brothers Titus 1992		
	Bo Jackson Baseball Data East 1991		
	Bomberman Hudson Soft 1989		
	Bomberman II Hudson Soft 1993		
	Bonk´s Adventure Hudson Soft 1994		
	Boulder Dash JVC 1990		
	Boy and his Blob, A Absolute 1990		
	Bram Stoker´s Dracula Sony 1993		
	Break Time - The National Pool Tour FCI 1993		
	Break Thru Data East 1987		
	Bubble Bobble Taito Software 1988		
	Bubble Bobble II Taito Software 1993		
	Bucky o´Hara Konami 1992		
	Bugs Bunny Crazy Castle Seika 1989		
	Bugs Bunny Birthday Blowout Seika 1990		
	Bump´n´Jump Vic Tokai 1988		
	Burai Fighter Taxan 1990		

Modul	Name	Inlay	OVP
	Burgertime Data East 1987		
	Cabal Milton Bradley 1989		
	Caesar´s Palace Virgin 1992		
	California Games Milton Bradley 1989		
	Captain America and the Avengers Data East 1991		
	Captain Planet Mindscape 1991		
	Captain Skyhawk Milton Bradley 1990		
	Casino Kid Sofel 1989		
	Casino Kid 2 Sofel 1993		
	Castelian Triffix 1991		
	Castle of Dragon Seta 1990		
	Castlequest Ascii 1989		
	Castlevania Konami 1987		
	Castlevania II - Simon´s Quest Konami 1988		
	Castlevania III - Dracula´s Curse Konami 1990		
	Caveman Games Data East 1990		
	Championship Bowling Romstar 1989		
	Championship Pool Mindscape 1993		

Modul	Name	Inlay	OVP
	Chessmaster Hi-Teck 1990		
	Chip ´n Dale- Rescue Rangers Capcom 1990		
	Chip ´n Dale- Rescue Rangers 2 Capcom 1994		
	Chubby Cherub Bandai 1986		
	Circus Caper Toho 1990		
	City Connection Jaleco 1988		
	Clash at Demonhead Vic Tokai 1990		
	Classic Concentration Gametek 1990		
	Cliffhanger Sony 1993		
	Clu Clu Land Nintendo 1985		
	Cobra Command Data East 1988		
	Cobra Triangle Nintendo 1989		
	Code Name: Viper Capcom 1990		
	Color a Dinosaur Virgin 1993		
	Commando Capcom 1986		
	Conan - The Mysteries of Time Mindscape 1991		
	Conan - The Mysteries of Time Mindscape 1991		
	Conquest of the Crystal Palace Asmik 1990		

Modul	Name	Inlay	OVP
	Contra Konami 1988		
	Contra Force Konami 1992		
	Cool World Ocean 1993		
	Cowboy Kid Romstar 1992		
	Crash´n Boys: Street Challenge American Technos 1992		
	Crystalis SNK 1990		
	Cybernoid - The Fighting Machine Acclaim 1989		
	Dance Aerobics Nintendo 1989		
	Danny Sullivan´s Indy Heat Tradewest 1992		
	Darkman Ocean 1991		
	Darkwing Duck Capcom 1992		
	Dash Galaxy in the Alien Asylum Data East 1990		
	Day Dreamin´Davey Hal America 1992		
	Days of Thunder Mindscape 1990		
	Deadly Towers Broderbund 1987		
	Defender II Hal America 1988		
	Defender of the Crown Ultra Soft 1989		
	Defenders of Dynatron City JVC 1992		

Modul	Name	Inlay	OVP
	Deja Vu Seika 1990		
	Demon Sword Taito Software 1990		
	Desert Commander Seika 1989		
	Destination Earth Star Acclaim 1990		
	Destiny of an Emperor Capcom 1990		
	Dick Tracy Bandai 1990		
	Die Hard Activision 1992		
	Dig Dug II Bandai 1989		
	Digger T. Rock - Legend of the Lost City Milton Bradley 1990		
	Dirty Harry - The War Against Drugs Mindscape 1990		
	Donkey Kong Nintendo 1986		
	Donkey Kong 3 Nintendo 1986		
	Donkey Kong Classics Nintendo 1988		
	Donkey Kong Jr. Nintendo 1986		
	Donkey Kong Jr. Math Nintendo 1985		
	Double Dare Gametek 1990		
	Double Dragon Tradewest 1988		
	Double Dragon II - The Revenge Acclaim 1990		

Modul	Name	Inlay	OVP
	Double Dragon Tradewest 1988		
	Double Dragon II - The Revenge Acclaim 1990		
	Double Dragon III - The Sacred Stone Acclaim 1991		
	Double Dribble Konami 1987		
	Dr. Chaos FCI 1988		
	Dr. Jekyll & Mr. Hyde Bandai 1989		
	Dr. Mario Nintendo 1990		
	Dragon Fighter Sofel 1992		
	Dragon Power Bandai 1988		
	Dragon Spirit - The New Legend Bandai 1990		
	Dragon Warrior Nintendo 1989		
	Dragon Warrior II Enix 1990		
	Dragon Warrior III Enix 1992		
	Dragon Warrior IV Enix 1992		
	Dragon's Lair Sony 1990		
	Duck Hunt Nintendo 1985		
	Duck Tales Capcom 1989		
	Duck Tales II Capcom 1993		

Modul	Name	Inlay	OVP
	Dungeon Magic Taito Software 1990		
	Dusty Diamond´s All-Star Softball Broderbund 1990		
	Dynowarz - The Destruction of Spondylus Bandai 1990		
	Elevator Action Taito Software 1987		
	Eliminator Boat Duel Electro Brain 1991		
	Empire Strikes Back, The JVC 1992		
	Evert & Lendl Top Player´s Tennis Asmik 1990		
	Excitebike Nintendo 1985		
	F-117A Stealth Fighter Microprose 1992		
	F-15 Strike Eagle Microprose 1992		
	Family Feud Gametek 1991		
	Faria - A World of Mystery & Danger Ascii 1991		
	Faxanadu Nintendo 1989		
	Felix the Cat Hudson Soft 1992		
	Ferrari Grand Prix Challenge Acclaim 1992		
	Fester´s Quest Sunsoft 1989		
	Final Fantasy Nintendo 1990		
	Fire ´N Ice Tecmo 1993		

Modul	Name	Inlay	OVP
	Fisher Price - Firehouse Rescue Gametek 1992		
	Fisher Price - I can remember Gametek 1990		
	Fisher Price - Perfect Fit Gametek 1990		
	Fist of the North Star Taxan 1989		
	Flight of the Intruder Mindscape 1991		
	Flinstones, The Taito Software 1991		
	Flinstones, The - The Surprise at Dinosaur Peak Taito Software 1994		
	Flying Dragon - The Secret Scroll Culture Brain 1989		
	Flying Warriors Culture Brain 1991		
	Formula 1 - Built to win Seta 1990		
	Frankenstein - The Monster Returns Bandai 1991		
	Freedom Force Sunsoft 1988		
	Friday the 13th LJN 1989		
	Fun House Hi-Teck 1991		
	G.I. Joe Taxan 1991		
	G.I. Joe - The Atlantis Factor Capcom 1992		
	Galaga Bandai 1988		
	Galaxy 5000 Activision 1991		

Modul	Name	Inlay	OVP
	Gargoyle´s Quest II Capcom 1992		
	Gauntlet II Mindscape 1990		
	Gemfire Koei 1992		
	Genghis Khan Koei 1990		
	George Foreman´s KO Boxing Acclaim 1992		
	Ghostbusters Activision 1988		
	Ghostbusters I Activision 1990		
	Ghost´n Goblins Capcom 1986		
	Ghoul School Electro Brain 1992		
	Goal ! Jaleco 1989		
	Goal ! 2 Jaleco 1992		
	Godzilla Toho 1989		
	Godzilla II - War of the Monsters Toho 1992		
	Gold Medal Challenge 92 Capcom 1992		
	Golf Nintendo 1985		
	Golf Grand Slam Atlus Software 1991		
	Golgo 13 - Top Secret Episode Vic Tokai 1988		
	Goonies II, The Konami 1987		

Modul	Name	Inlay	OVP
	Gotcha LJN 1987		
	Gradius Konami 1986		
	Great Waldo Search, The THQ 1992		
	Greg Norman´s Golf Power Virgin 1992		
	Gremlins2 - The New Batch Sunsoft 1990		
	Guardian Legend, The Broderbund 1989		
	Guerilla War SNK 1989		
	Gumshoe Nintendo 1986		
	Gun Nac Ascii 1991		
	Gunsmoke Capcom 1988		
	Gyromite Nintendo 1985		
	Gyruss Ultra Soft 1989		
	Harlem Globetrotters Gametek 1991		
	Hatris Bullet Proof Software 1992		
	Heavy Barrel Data East 1990		
	Heavy Shreddin´ Parker Brothers 1990		
	High Speed Tradewest 1991		
	Hogan´s Alley Nintendo 1985		

Modul	Name	Inlay	OVP
	Hollywood Squares Gametek 1989		
	Home Alone THQ 1991		
	Home Alone 2 - Lost in New York THQ 1992		
	Hook Sony 1992		
	Hoops Jaleco 1989		
	Hudson Hawk Sony 1992		
	Hunt for Red October, The Hi-Tech 1991		
	Hydlide FCI 1989		
	Ice Climber Nintendo 1985		
	Ice Hockey Nintendo 1988		
	Ikari Warrios SNK 1987		
	Ikari Warrios II - Victory Road SNK 1988		
	Ikari Warrios III - The Rescue SNK 1991		
	Image Fight Irem 1990		
	Immortal, The EA 1990		
	Incedible Crash Dummies, The LJN 1994		
	Indiana Jones and the Last Crusade Taito Software 1991 - UBI Soft 1993		
	Indiana Jones and the Temple of Doom Mindscape 1988		

Modul	Name	Inlay	OVP
	John Infiltrator Mindscape 1990		
	Iron Tank SNK 1988		
	Iron Sword - Wizards and Warriors II Acclaim 1989		
	Isolated Warrior NTVIC 1991		
	Ivan - Iron Man - Stewart´s Super Off Road Tradewest 1990		
	Jack Nicklaus Major Championship Golf Konami 1990		
	Jackal Konami 1988		
	Jackie Chan´s Action Kung Fu Hudson Soft 1990		
	James Bond Jr. THQ 1992		
	Jaws LJN 1987		
	Jeopardy Gametek 1988		
	Jeopardy - 25th. Silver Anniversary Edition Gametek 1990		
	Jeopardy - Jr. Edition Gametek 1989		
	Jetsons - Cogswell´s Caper Taito Software 1992		
	Jimmy Connors Pro Tennis Tour UBi Soft 1993		
	Joe & Mac Data East 1992		
	John Elway´s Quarterback Tradewest 1989		
	Jordan vs. Bird - One on One Milton Bradley 1989		

Modul	Name	Inlay	OVP
	Journey to Silius Sunsoft 1990		
	Joust Hal America 1988		
	Jungle Book, The Virgin 1994		
	Jurrasic Park Ocean 1993		
	Kabuki - Quantum Fighter Hal America 1991		
	Karate Champ Data East 1986		
	Karate Kid LJN 1987		
	Karnov Data East 1988		
	Kick Master Taito Software 1992		
	Kickle Cubicle Irem 1990		
	Kid Icarus Nintendo 1987		
	Kid Klown in Night Mayor World Kemco 1993		
	Kid Kool Vic Tokai 1990		
	Kid Niki Data East 1987		
	King´s Knight Square Soft 1989		
	Kings of the Beach Ultra Soft 1990		
	King´s Quest V Konami 1992		
	Kirby´s Adventure Nintendo 1993		

Modul	Name	Inlay	OVP
	Kiwi Kraze Taito Software 1991		
	Klashball Sofel 1991		
	Knight Rider Acclaim 1989		
	Krion Conquest, The Vic Tokai 1991		
	Krusty´s Funhouse Acclaim 1992		
	Kung Fu Nintendo 1985		
	Kung Fu Heroes Culture Brain 1989		
	Laser Invasion Ultra Soft 1991		
	Last Action Hero Sony 1993		
	Last Ninja, The Jaleco 1991		
	Last Starfighter, The Mindscape 1990		
	Lee Trevino´s Fighting Golf SNK 1988		
	Legacy of the Wizard, The Broderbund 1989		
	Legend of Ghost Lion Kemco 1992		
	Legend of Kage, The Taito Software 1987		
	Legend of Zelda, The Nintendo 1987		
	Legendary Wings Capcom 1988		
	Legends of the Diamond Bandai 1992		

Modul	Name	Inlay	OVP
	Lemmings Sunsoft 1992		
	LÉmpereur Koei 1991		
	Lethal Weapon Ocean 1993		
	Life Force Konami 1988		
	Little League Baseball - Championship Series SNK 1990		
	Little Mermaid Capcom 1991		
	Little Nemo - The Dream Master Capcom 1990		
	Little Ninja Brothers Culture Brain 1990		
	Little Samson Taito Software 1992		
	Lode Runner Broderbund 1987		
	Lone Ranger, The Konami 1991		
	Loopz Mindscape 1990		
	Low G-Man Taxan 1990		
	Lunar Pool FCI 1987		
	M.C. Kids Virgin 1992		
	M.U.L.E. Mindscape 1990		
	M.U.S.C.L.E. Bandai 1986		
	Mach Rider Nintendo 1985		

Modul	Name	Inlay	OVP
	Mad Max Mindscape 1990		
	Mafat Conspiracy - Golgo 13 II, The Vic Tokai 1990		
	Magic Darts Romstar 1991		
	Magic Johnson´s Fast Break Tradewest 1990		
	Magic of Scheherazade Culture Brain 1989		
	Magician Taxan 1991		
	Magmax FCI 1988		
	Major League Baseball LJN 1988		
	Maniac Mansion Jaleco 1990		
	Mappyland Taxan 1989		
	Marble Madness Milton Bradley 1989		
	Mario Bros. Nintendo 1986		
	Mario is Missing Mindscape 1993		
	Mario´s Time Machine Mindscape 1994		
	Marvel´s X-Men LJN 1989		
	Mechanized Attack SNK 1990		
	Mega Man Campcom 1987		
	Mega Man 2 Capcom 1989		

Modul	Name	Inlay	OVP
	Mega Man 3 Capcom 1990		
	Mega Man 4 Capcom 1992		
	Mega Man 5 Capcom 1992		
	Mega Man 6 Nintendo 1994		
	Mendel Palace Hudson Soft 1990		
	Metal Gear Ultra Soft 1988		
	Metal Mech Jaleco 1991		
	Metal Storm Irem 1991		
	Metroid Nintendo 1986		
	Michael Andretti´s World Grand Prix American Sammy 1990		
	Mickey Mousecapades Capcom 1988		
	Mickeys Adventures in Numberland Hi-Tech 1994		
	Mickeys Safari in Letterland Hi-Tech 1993		
	Might & Magic - Secret of the Inner Sanctum American Sammy 1992		
	Mighty Bomb Jack Tecmo 1987		
	Mighty Final Fight Capcom 1993		
	Millipede Hal America 1988		
	Milon´s Secret Castle Hudson Soft 1988		

Modul	Name	Inlay	OVP
	Mission Impossible Ultra Soft 1990		
	Monopoly Parker Brothers 1991		
	Monster in my Pocket Konami 1992		
	Monster Party Bandai 1989		
	Monster Truck Rally INTV 1991		
	Motor City Patrol Matchbox Toys 1992		
	Ms. Pac Man Namco 1993		
	Muppet Adventure - Chaos at the Carneval Hi-Tech 1990		
	Mutant Virus, The American Softworks 1992		
	Mystery Quest Taxan 1989		
	NARC Acclaim 1990		
	NES Open Tournament Golf Nintendo 1991		
	NES Play Action Football Nintendo 1990		
	NFL Football LJN 1989		
	Nigel Mansell´s World Championship Racing Gametek 1993		
	Nightshade Ultra Soft 1992		
	Ninja Crusaders American Sammy 1990		
	Ninja Gaiden Tecmo 1989		

Modul	Name	Inlay	OVP
	Ninja Gaiden II - The Dark Sword of Chaos Tecmo 1990		
	Ninja Gaiden III - The Ancient Ship of Doom Tecmo 1991		
	Ninja Kid Bandai 1986		
	Nintendo World Cup Soccer Nintendo 1990		
	Nobuanga´s Ambition Koei 1989		
	Nobuanga´s Ambition II Koei 1991		
	North and South Seika 1990		
	Operation Wolf Taito Software 1989		
	Orb-3D Hi-Tech 1990		
	Othello Acclaim 1988		
	Overlord Virgin 1993		
	P.O.W. - Prisoners of War SNK 1989		
	Pac Man Namco 1993		
	Palamedes Hot-B 1990		
	Panic Restaurant Taito Software 1992		
	Paperboy Mindscape 1988		
	Paperboy 2 Mindscape 1992		
	Peter Pan & the Pirates THQ 1991		

Modul	Name	Inlay	OVP
	Phantom Fighter FCI 1990		
	Pictionary LJN 1990		
	Pinball Nintendo 1985		
	Pinball Quest Jaleco 1990		
	Pinbot Nintendo 1990		
	Pipe Dream Bullet Proof Software 1990		
	Pirates Ultra Soft 1991		
	Platoon Sunsoft 1988		
	Popeye Nintendo 1986		
	Power Blade Taito Software 1991		
	Power Blade 2 Taito Software 1992		
	Power Punch II American Softworks 1992		
	Predator Activision 1989		
	Prince of Persia Virgin 1992		
	Princess Tomato in the Salad Kingdom Hudson Soft 1991		
	Pro Sport Hockey Jaleco 1993		
	Pro Wrestling Nintendo 1987		
	Punch-Out! Feat. Mr. Dream Nintendo 1987		

Modul	Name	Inlay	OVP
	Punisher, The LJN 1990		
	Puss´N Boots - Pero´s Great Adventure Electro Brain 1990		
	Puzznic Taito Software 1990		
	Q-Bert Ultra Soft 1989		
	Qix Taito Software 1991		
	R.C. Pro-Am II Tradewest 1992		
	R.C. Pro-Am Racing Nintendo 1988		
	Race America Absolute 1992		
	Racket Attack Jaleco 1988		
	Rad Racer Nintendo 1987		
	Rad Racer II Square Soft 1990		
	Raid on Bungeling Bay Broderbund 1987		
	Rainbow Islands Taito Software 1991		
	Rally Bike Romstar 1990		
	Rambo Acclaim 1988		
	Rampage Data East 1988		
	Rampart Jaleco 1992		
	Remote Control Hi-Tech 1990		

Modul	Name	Inlay	OVP
	Ren & Stimpy Show - Buckaroos, The THQ 1993		
	Renegade Taito Software 1988		
	Rescue - The Embassy Mission Seika 1990		
	Ring King Data East 1987		
	River City Ransom American Technos 1990		
	Roadblasters Mindscape 1990		
	Robin Hood - Prince of Thieves Virgin 1991		
	RoboCop Data East 1989		
	RoboCop 2 Data East 1991		
	RoboCop 3 Ocean 1992		
	Robowarrior Jaleco 1988		
	Rock'n Ball NTVIC 1990		
	Rocket Ranger Seika 1990		
	Rocketeer, The Bandai 1991		
	Rockin'Kats Atlus Software 1991		
	Roger Clemens MVP Baseball LJN 1991		
	Rollerball Hal America 1990		
	Rollerblade Racer Hi-Tech 1993		

Modul	Name	Inlay	OVP
	Rollergames Ultra Soft 1990		
	Romance of the three Kingdoms Koei 1989		
	Romance of the three Kingdoms II Koei 1991		
	Roundball - 2 on 2 Challenge Mindscape 1992		
	Rush´n Attack Konami 1987		
	Rygar Tecmo 1987		
	S.C.A.T. - Special Cybernetic Attack Team Natsume 1991		
	Section Z Capcom 1987		
	Seicross FCI 1988		
	Sesame Street 123 Hi-Tech 1989		
	Sesame Street ABC Hi-Tech 1989		
	Sesame Street ABC / 123 Hi-Tech 1991		
	Sesame Street Big Bird´s Hide & Speak Hi-Tech 1990		
	Sesame Street - Countdown Hi-Tech 1992		
	Shadow of the Ninja Natsume 1990		
	Shadowgate Seika 1989		
	Shatterhand Jaleco 1991		
	Shingen the Ruler Hot-B 1990		

Modul	Name	Inlay	OVP
	Shooting Range Bandai 1989		
	Short Order/Eggsplode Nintendo 1989		
	Side Pocket Data East 1987		
	Silent Service Ultra Soft 1989		
	Silkworm American Sammy 1990		
	Silver Surfer Virgin 1990		
	Simpsons - Bart vs the Space Mutants Acclaim 1991		
	Simpsons - Bart vs the World Acclaim 1991		
	Simpsons - Bartman meets Radioactive Man Acclaim 1992		
	Skate or Die Ultra Soft 1988		
	Skate or Die 2 EA 1990		
	Ski or Die Ultra Soft 1991		
	Sky Kid Sunsoft 1987		
	Sky Shark Taito Software 1989		
	Slalom Nintendo 1987		
	Smash T.V. Acclaim 1991		
	Snake Rattle ´n Roll Nintendo 1990		
	Snake´s Revenge - Metal Gear II Ultra Soft 1990		

NES 31

Modul	Name	Inlay	OVP
	Snoopy´s Silly Sports Spectacular Seika 1990		
	Snow Brothers Capcom 1991		
	Soccer Nintendo 1987		
	Solar Jetman - Hunt for the golden Warship Tradewest 1990		
	Solomon´s Key Tecmo 1987		
	Solstice Sony 1990		
	Space Shuttle Project Absolute 1991		
	Spelunker Broderbund 1987		
	Spider-Man - Return of the Sinister Six LJN 1992		
	Spot Virgin 1990		
	Spy Hunter Sunsoft 1987		
	Spy vs. Spy Seika 1988		
	Sqoon Irem 1987		
	Stack-Up Nintendo 1985		
	Stadium Events Bandai 1987		
	Stanley an the search for Dr. Livingston Electro Brain 1992		
	Star Force Tecmo 1987		
	Star Soldier Taxan 1989		

Modul	Name	Inlay	OVP
	Star Trek Ultra Soft 1992		
	Star Trek - The next Generation Abolute 1993		
	Star Voyager Acclaim 1987		
	Star Wars JVC 1991		
	Starship Hector Hudson Soft 1990		
	Star Tropics Nintendo 1990		
	Stealth ATV Activision 1989		
	Stinger Konami 1987		
	Street Cop Bandai 1989		
	Street Fighter 2010 - The Final Fight Capcom 1990		
	Strider Capcom 1989		
	Super C Konami 1990		
	Super Cars Electro Brain 1991		
	Super Dodge Ball Sony 1989		
	Super Glove Ball Mattel 1990		
	Super Jeopardy! Gametek 1991		
	Super Mario Bros. Nintendo 1985		
	Super Mario Bros. 2 Nintendo 1988		

Modul	Name	Inlay	OVP
	Super Mario Bros. 3 Nintendo 1990		
	Super Pitfall Activision 1987		
	Super Spike V-Ball Nintendo 1990		
	Super Spy Hunter Sunsoft 1992		
	Super Team Games Nintendo 1988		
	Superman Seika 1988		
	Swamp Thing THQ 1992		
	Sword Master Activision 1992		
	Swords and Serpents Acclaim 1990		
	Taboo - The sixth Sense Tradewest 1989		
	Tag Team Wrestling Data East 1986		
	Tale Spin Capcom 1991		
	Target - Renegade Taito Software 1990		
	Tecmo Baseball Tecmo 1989		
	Tecmo Bowl Tecmo 1989		
	Tecmo NBA Basketball Tecmo 1992		
	Tecmo Super Bowl Tecmo 1991		
	Tecmo World Cup Soccer Tecmo 1992		

NES 34

Modul	Name	Inlay	OVP
	Tecmo World Wrestling Tecmo 1990		
	Teenage Mutant Ninja Turtles Ultra Soft 1989		
	Teenage Mutant Ninja Turtles 2 - The Arcade Game Ultra Soft 1990		
	Teenage Mutant Ninja Turtles 3 - The Manhattan Project Ultra Soft 1992		
	Teenage Mutant Ninja Turtles - Tournament Fighters Konami 1994		
	Tennis Nintendo 1985		
	Terminator Mindscape 1992		
	Terminator 2 - Judgment Day Acclaim 1992		
	Terra Cresta Vic Tokai 1990		
	Tetris Nintendo 1989		
	Tetris 2 Nintendo 1993		
	Three Stooges, The Activision 1989		
	Thunder & Lightning Romstar 1990		
	Thunderbirds Activision 1990		
	Thundercade American Sammy 1989		
	Tiger-Heli Acclaim 1987		

Modul	Name	Inlay	OVP
	Time Lord Milton Bradley 1990		
	Times of Lore Toho 1991		
	Tiny Toon Adventures Konami 1991		
	Tiny Toon Adventures 2 - Trouble in Wackyland Konami 1993		
	Tiny Toon Adventures Cartoon Workshop Konami 1992		
	To the Earth Nintendo 1989		
	Toki Taito Software 1991		
	Tom & Jerry Hi-Tech 1991		
	Tombs & Treasure Activision 1991		
	Top Gun Konami 1987		
	Top Gun - The second Mission Konami 1990		
	Total Recall Acclaim 1990		
	Totally Rad Jaleco 1991		
	Touchdown Fever SNK 1991		
	Town & Country Surf Designs LJN 1988		
	Town & Country II - Thrilla's Surfari Acclaim 1992		
	Toxic Crusaders Bandai 1992		
	Track & Field Konami 1987		

Modul	Name	Inlay	OVP
	Track & Field II Konami 1989		
	Treasure Master American Softworks 1991		
	Trog Acclaim 1991		
	Trojan Capcom 1987		
	Twin Cobra American Sammy 1990		
	Twin Eagle Romstar 1989		
	Ultima - Exodus FCI 1989		
	Ultima - Quest of the Avatar FCI 1990		
	Ultima - Warriors of Destiny FCI 1993		
	Ultimate Air Combat Activision 1992		
	Ultimate Basketball American Sammy 1990		
	Uncharted Waters Koei 1991		
	Uninvited Seika 1991		
	Untouchables, The Ocean 1991		
	Urban Champion Nintendo 1986		
	Vegas Dream Hal America 1990		
	Vice - Project Doom American Sammy 1991		
	Videomation THQ 1991		

Modul	Name	Inlay	OVP
	Volleyball Nintendo 1987		
	Wacky Races Atlus Software 1992		
	Wall Street Kid Sofel 1990		
	Wario´s Woods Nintendo 1994		
	Wayne Gretzky Hockey THQ 1991		
	Wayne´s World THQ 1993		
	Werewolf - The last Warrior Data East 1990		
	Wheel of Fortune Ganetek 1988		
	Wheel of Fortune - Family Edition Ganetek 1990		
	Wheel of Fortune - Feat. Vanna White Ganetek 1992		
	Wheel of Fortune Jr. Ganetek 1989		
	Where´s Waldo ? THQ 1991		
	Who Framed Roger Rabbit LJN 1989		
	Whomp Ém Jaleco 1991		
	Widget Atlus Software 1992		
	Wild Gunman Nintendo 1985		
	Willow Capcom 1989		
	Win, Lose or Draw Hie-Tech 1990		

Modul	Name	Inlay	OVP
	Winter Games Acclaim 1987		
	Wizardry - Proving Grounds of the Mad Overlord - Ascii 1990		
	Wizardry II - Knights of Diamonds Ascii 1992		
	Wizards & Warriors Acclaim 1987		
	Wizards & Warriors III Acclaim 1992		
	Wolverine LJN 1991		
	World Champ Romstar 1991		
	World Championship Wrestling FCI 1990		
	World Class Track Meet Nintendo 1988		
	World Games Milton Bradley 1989		
	Wrath of the black Manta Taito Software 1990		
	Wrecking Crew Nintendo 1985		
	Wrestle Mania Acclaim 1989		
	Wurm - Journey to the Center of the Earth Asmik 1991		
	WWF Wrestlemania Challenge LJN 1990		
	WWF Wrestlemania - Steel Cage Challenge Acclaim 1992		
	WWF King of the Ring LJN 1993		
	Xenophobe Sunsoft 1988		

Modul	Name	Inlay	OVP
	Xevious Bandai 1988		
	Xexyz Hudson Soft 1990		
	Yo! Noid Capcom 1990		
	Yoshi Nintendo 1992		
	Yoshi´s Cookie Nintendo 1993		
	Young Indiana Jones Chronicles, The Jaleco 1992		
	Zanac FCI 1987		
	Zelda II - The Adventure of Link Nintendo 1988		
	Zen - Intergalactic Ninja Konami 1993		
	Zoda´s Revenge - Star Tropics II Nintendo 1994		
	Zombie Nation Meldac 1991		

SNES Super Nintendo Entertainment System (c)

Technische Daten: 16 Bit Videospielkonsole
Auflösung: 256 - 512 Pixel
RAM: 128 KB
CPU: 3,5 MHz
Speichermedium: Modul (32 Mbit)
Verkaufszeitraum Europa: 1992 bis 1998
Verkaufte Einheiten: 49 Millionen weltweit

Zubehör:
- Gameboyadapter
- Super 8 TriStar - NES Adapter
- Importadapter für PAL und/oder NTSC Spiele
- Super Scope - Lightgun
- Multitap - Adapter für bis zu 5 Controller
- SNES Maus
- Score master - Super Advantage - Joyboard

Modul	Name	Inlay	OVP
	90 Minutes European Prime Goal Ocean 1995		
	AAAHHIII Real Monsters Viacom New Media 1995		
	ACME Animation Factory Sunsoft 1994		
	Act Raiser Enix 1990		
	Act Raiser 2 Enix 1993		
	Addams Family Ocean 1992		
	Addams Family Values Ocean 1994		
	Addams Family Pugsleys Scavenger Hunt Ocean 1993		
	Adventures of Batman & Robin Konami 1995		
	Adventures of Dr. Franken DTMC 1994		
	Adventures of Mighty Max Ocean 1995		
	Aero the Acro-Bat Sunsoft 1993		
	Aero the Acro-Bat 2 Sunsoft 1994		
	Aguri Suzuki F1 Super Driving Altron 1992		
	Air Cavalry Gametek 1995		
	Al Unser Jr´s Road to the Top Gametek 1995		
	Adventure Island Hudson Soft 1992		
	Alfred Chicken Mindscape 1994		

Modul	Name	Inlay	OVP
	Alien 3 Acclaim Entertainment 1993		
	Alien vs. Predator Activision 1993		
	All American Championship Football THQ 1994		
	An American Tail Fievel goes West Hudson Soft 1994		
	Animaniacs Konami 1994		
	Another World Delphine Software 1992		
	Arcades Greatest Hits, Williams Williams 1996		
	Arcades Greatest Hits - Atari Collection 1 Midway 1997		
	Archer Maclean´s Super Dropzone Psygnosis 1994		
	Ardy Lightfoot Titus 1994		
	Arkanoid Nintendo 1997		
	Art of Fighting SNK 1992		
	Asterix Inforgrames 1993		
	Asterix & Obelix Inforgrames 1993		
	Axelay Sunsoft 1993		
	B.O.B. EA 1993		
	Barkley Shut Up And Jump Sony 1994		
	Bass Masters Classic Pro Malibu 1996		

SNES 43

Modul	Name	Inlay	OVP
	Batman forever Acclaim 1995		
	Batman returns Konami 1993		
	Battle Clash Nintendo 1993		
	Battletoads & Double Dragon Nintendo 1993		
	Battletoads & Battlemaniacs Tradewest 1993		
	Beavis and Butt-Head Viacom 1995		
	Beethoven - The Ultimate Canine Caper Hi-Tech 1994		
	Best of the best - Championship Karate Electrobrain 1992		
	Big Sky Trooper JVC 1995		
	Biker Mice from Mars Konami 1994		
	Bio Metal Activision 1993		
	Black Hawk Interplay 1994		
	Blazing Skies Namco 1993		
	Blues Brothers, The Titus 1992		
	Boogerman Interplay 1996		
	Bomberman Hudson Soft 1993		
	Bomberman 2 Nintendo 1995		
	Bomberman 3 Hudson Soft 1995		

Modul	Name	Inlay	OVP
	Boxing Legends of the Ring Electro Brain 1993		
	Brainers, The Titus 1996		
	Brawl Brothers Jaleco 1993		
	Breath of Fire 2 Capcom 1994		
	Brett Hull Hockey Accolade 1995		
	Brutal Paws of Fury Gametek 1994		
	Bubsy - Claws Encounters of the furred Kind Accolade 1996		
	Bubsy 2 Accolade 1994		
	Bugs Bunny Rabbit Rampage Sunsoft 1994		
	Bulls vs. Blazers and the NBA Playoffs EA 1992		
	Cal Ripken Jr. Baseball Mindscape 1993		
	California Games 2 Image Soft 1993		
	Cannon Fodder Virgin 1994		
	Captain America and the Avengers Mindscape 1993		
	Captain Commando Capcom 1995		
	Carrier Aces Gametek 1995		
	Casper Natsume 1996		
	Castlevenia 4 Konami 1992		

Modul	Name	Inlay	OVP
	Castlevenia Vampires Kiss Konami 1995		
	Champions World Class Soccer Acclaim 1994		
	Championship Pool Mindscape 1993		
	Chaos Engine, The Renegade 1993		
	Chessmaster, The Software Toolworks 1991		
	Choplifter Ocean 1994		
	Chuck Rock Virgin 1992		
	Clay Fighter Interplay Entertainment 1994		
	Clay Fighter 2 - Judgement Clay Interplay Entertainment 1995		
	Claymates Interplay Entertainment 1993		
	Cliffhanger Sony 1993		
	Congos Caper Data East 1993		
	Cool Spot Virgin 1994		
	Cool World Ocean 1992		
	Cutthroat Island Acclaim 1995		
	Cybernator Konami 1993		
	Daffy Duck - The Marvin Missions Sunsoft 1994		
	Darius Twin Square Enix 1991		

Modul	Name	Inlay	OVP
	David Cranes Amazing Tennis Absolut Entertainment 1992		
	Daze before Christmas Sunsoft 1994		
	Death and the Return of Superman, The Sunsoft 1994		
	Demolition Man Acclaim 1995		
	Demons Crest Capcom 1995		
	Dennis Ocean 1993		
	Desert Fighter Seta 1994		
	Desert Strike - Return to the Gulf EA 1992		
	Dino City Irem 1992		
	Dino Dinis Soccer Virgin 1994		
	Dirtracer Elite Systems 1995		
	Dirt Trax FX Acclaim 1995		
	Disney Beauty and the Beast Probe Entertainment 1994		
	Disney Pinocchio Virgin 1996		
	Disney Toy Story Capcom 1995		
	Disney Timon & Pumbas Jungle Games THQ 1997		
	Disney Dschungelbuch Virgin 1994		
	Disney Goof Troop Capcom 1993		

Modul	Name	Inlay	OVP
	Disney Aladdin Capcom 1993		
	Disney König der Löwen Virgin 1994		
	Disney Maui Mallard - Donald Nintendo 1996		
	Donkey Kong Country Nintendo 1994		
	Donkey Kong Country 2 - Diddy's Kong Quest Nintendo 1995		
	Donkey Kong Country 3 - Dixie Kong's Double Trouble Nintendo 1996		
	Doom Williams 1995		
	Double Dragon 5 - The Shadow Falls Tradewest 1994		
	Dracula Psygnosis 1993		
	Dragon Ball Z - Hyper Dimension Bandai 1996		
	Dragon Ball Z - La Legende Saien Bandai 1994		
	Dragon Ball Z - Super Butouden Bandai 1993		
	Dragon Ball Z - Ultime Menace Bandai 1994		
	Dragon's Lair Data East 1993		
	Dragon - The Bruce Lee Story Acclaim 1995		
	Drakkhen Seika Corp. 1991		
	Dungeon Master Victor 1993		

Modul	Name	Inlay	OVP
	Earth Defense Force Jaleco 1992		
	Earthworm Jim Playmates 1994		
	Earthworm Jim 2 Playmates 1995		
	Eekl the Cat Ocean 1994		
	Equinox Epic Sony Record 1994		
	Eric Cantona Football Challenge Rage Software 1993		
	ESPN Baseball Tonight Sony 1994		
	EURO Football Champ Taito 1992		
	Exhaust Heat Ocean 1992		
	F-Zero Nintendo 1991		
	F1 Pole Position Ubisoft 1993		
	F1 Pole Position 2 Ubisoft 1993		
	F1 World Championship Edition Acclaim 1995		
	Family Dog Malibu 1993		
	Fatal Fury Takara 1993		
	Fatal Fury 2 Takara 1994		
	Fatal Fury Special Takara 1995		
	Fever Pitch Soccer U.S. Gold 1995		

SNES 49

Modul	Name	Inlay	OVP
	FIFA International Soccer EA 1994		
	FIFA Soccer 96 EA 1995		
	FIFA Soccer 97 EA 1996		
	FIFA Road to World Cup 98 EA 1998		
	Final Fight Capcom 1991		
	Final Fight 2 Capcom 1993		
	Final Fight 3 Capcom 1996		
	First Samurai Kemco 1993		
	Flashback Sunsoft 1993		
	Flinstones, The Ocean 1995		
	Foreman for Real Acclaim 1995		
	Frank Thomas Big Hurt Baseball Acclaim 1995		
	Frantic Flea Gametek 1996		
	Full Throttle all American Racing Cybersoft 1995		
	Fun 'n Games - Paint - Games - Music Tradewest 1994		
	Garry Kitchen's Super Battletank Absolute Entertainment 1992		
	Georg Foreman's KO Boxing Acclaim 1992		
	Ghoul Patrol JVC 1994		

Modul	Name	Inlay	OVP
	Gods Mindscape 1992		
	GP-1 Atlus 1993		
	Great Circus Mystery Capcom 1994		
	Hagane - The final Conflict Hudson 1995		
	Hal's Hole in one Golf Hal Laboratory Inc. 1991		
	Harley's Humongous Adventures Hi Tech Expression 1993		
	Harvest Moon Natsume 1998		
	Hebereke's Popoitto Sunsoft 1995		
	Heberekes's Popoon Sunsoft 1994		
	Home Alone THQ 1991		
	Home Alone 2 - Lost in New York THQ 1992		
	Hook Sony 1992		
	Hungry Dinosaurs Sunsoft 1995		
	Hurricanes U.S. Gold 1994		
	Hyper V-Ball Mc O'River 1994		
	Hyper-Zone Hal Laboratory Inc. 1991		
	Illusions of TIME Nintendo 1995		
	Incantation Titus Software 1996		

Modul	Name	Inlay	OVP
	Incredible Crash Dummies, The LJN 1993		
	Indiana Jones Greatest Adventures JVC 1994		
	International Sensible Soccer Sony 1994		
	International Superstar Soccer Konami 1995		
	International Superstar Soccer Deluxe Konami 1995		
	International Tennis Tour Taito 1993		
	Izzy´s Quest for the Olympic Rings U.S.Gold 1995		
	Jack Nicklaus Golf Tradewest 1992		
	James Bond Jr. THQ 1992		
	James Pond´s Crazy Chase Sports Seika 1993		
	Jelly Boy Ocean 1995		
	Jimmy connors Pro Tennis Tour Ubisoft 1992		
	Joe & Mac 3 Data East 1994		
	Joe & Mac Caveman Ninja Elite 1992		
	John Madden Football 93 EA 1992		
	Judge Dredd Acclaim 1995		
	Jungle Strike EA 1995		
	Jurassic Park Ocean 1993		

Modul	Name	Inlay	OVP
	Jurassic Park 2 - The Chaos Continues Ocean 1994		
	Justice League Task Force Sunsoft 1995		
	Kawasaki Superbikes Time Warner Interaktive 1995		
	Kick Off Misawa 1993		
	Kick Off 4 Vic Tokai 1994		
	Kid Clown in crazy Chase Kemco 1994		
	Killer Instinct Nintendo 1995		
	King Arthurs World Jaleco 1993		
	King of Dragons Capcom 1994		
	King of Monsters Takara 1992		
	Kirby´s Dream Course Nintendo 1995		
	Kirby´s Dream Land 3 Nintendo 1997		
	Kirby´s Fun Park Nintendo 1996		
	Kirby´s Ghost Trap Nintendo 1995		
	Knights of the Round Capcom 1994		
	Krusty´s Super Fun House Acclaim 1992		
	Lagoon Kemco 1991		
	Lamborghini American Challenge Titus 1993		

Modul	Name	Inlay	OVP
	Last Action Hero Sony 1993		
	Lawnmower Man, The - Rasenmähermann THQ 1993		
	Legend Seika 1994		
	Lemmings Sunsoft 1992		
	Lemmings 2 - The Tribes Psygnosis 1994		
	Lethal Enforcers Konami 1994		
	Lethal Weapon Ocean 1992		
	Looney Tunes Basketball Sunsoft 1995		
	Looney Tunes Road Runner Sunsoft 1992		
	Lord of the Rings - Volume 1 Interplay 1994		
	Lost Vikings, The Interplay 1993		
	Lost Vikings 2, The - Norse by Norsewest Interplay 1997		
	Lothar Matthaeus Super Soccer Ocean 1995		
	Lucky Lucke Infogrames 1997		
	Lufia Natsume 1995		
	Madden 95 EA 1994		
	Madden NFL 94 EA 1993		
	Magic Boy JVC 1996		

Modul	Name	Inlay	OVP
	Magic Sword Capcom 1992		
	Magical Quest - Starring Mickey Mouse Capcom 1992		
	Major Title Irem 1992		
	Manchester United Championship Soccer Ocean 1995		
	Mario ist missing Software Toolworks 1993		
	Mario Paint Nintendo 1992		
	Mario´s Time Machine Mindscape 1993		
	Marko´s Magic Football Acclaim 1995		
	Marvel Super Heroes in War of the Gems Capcom 1996		
	Mask, The Black Pearl 1995		
	Mechwarrior Activison 1993		
	Mechwarrior 3050 Activision 1995		
	Mega Man 7 Capcom 1995		
	Mega Man X Capcom 1994		
	Mega Man X2 Capcom 1995		
	Mega Man X3 Capcom 1996		
	Mega-Lo-Mania Imagineer 1994		
	Metal Combat Falcon´s Revenge Nintendo 1993		

Modul	Name	Inlay	OVP
	Metal Marines Namco Bandai Games 1993		
	Michael Jordan Chaos in Windy City EA 1994		
	Mickey Mania Sony 1994		
	Micro Machines Ocean 1994		
	Micro Machines 2 Ocean 1996		
	Might & Magic 2 - Gates to another World Logic 1993		
	Mighty Morphin Power Rangers Fighting Edition Bandai 1995		
	Mighty Morphin Power Rangers - The Movie Bandai 1995		
	Mohawk & Headphone Jack Black Pearl 1996		
	Mortal Kombat Acclaim 1993		
	Mortal Kombat II Acclaim 1994		
	Mortal Kobat III Acclaim 1995		
	Mr. Do! Black Pearl 1996		
	Mr. Nutz Ocean 1994		
	Ms. Pac-Man Midway 1996		
	Mystic Quest Legend Square Soft 1992		
	NBA All-Star Challenge LJN 1992		

Modul	Name	Inlay	OVP
	NBA Hang Time Midway 1995		
	NBA Jam Acclaim 1994		
	NBA Jam Tournament Edition Acclaim 1995		
	NBA Live 95 EA 1994		
	NBA Live 96 EA 1995		
	NBA Live 97 EA 1996		
	Newmann Haas Indy Car Acclaim 1994		
	NFL Football Konami 1993		
	NFL Quarterback Club LJN 1994		
	NFL Quarterback Club 96 Acclaim 1995		
	NHL 95 EA 1994		
	NHL 96 EA 1995		
	NHL 97 EA 1996		
	NHL Hockey 94 EA 1993		
	NHLPA Hockey 93 EA 1992		
	Ninja Warriors New Generation Titus 1994		
	Olympic Summer Games Black Pearl 1996		
	On the Ball Taito 1992		

Modul	Name	Inlay	OVP
	Operation Starfisch James Pond 3 U.S.Gold 1994		
	Operation Logic Bomb Jaleco 1993		
	Oscar Titus 1996		
	Out to Lunch Pierre Le Chef Mindscape 1993		
	Outlander Mindscape 1993		
	Pac-Attack Namco 1993		
	Pac-In-Time Namco 1995		
	Pac-Man 2 - New Adventures Namco 1994		
	Pagemaster, The Fox Interactive 1994		
	Paperboy 2 Mindscape 1991		
	Parodius Non Sense Fantasy Konami 1992		
	Pebble Beach Golf Links T&E Soft 1992		
	PGA European Tour Black Pearl 1996		
	PGA Tour Black Pearl 1995		
	PGA Golf Tour EA 1992		
	Phalanx Kemco 1992		
	Phantom 2040 Viacom New Media 1995		
	Pilotwings Nintendo 1991		

Modul	Name	Inlay	OVP
	Pinball Dreams Gametek 1994		
	Pinball Fantasies Gametek 1995		
	Pink Goes to Hollywood TecMagic 1993		
	Pirates of dark Water, The Sunsoft 1994		
	Pit Fighter THQ 1992		
	Pitfall - The Mayan Adventure Activision 1994		
	Player Manager - Rummenigge Imagineer 1993		
	Player Manager - Keegan´s Imagineer 1993		
	Plok Tradewest 1993		
	Pocky & Rocky Natsume 1993		
	Pocky & Rocky 2 Ocean 1994		
	Pop´n Twin Bee Konami 1993		
	Pop´n Twin Bee - Rainbow Bell Adventures Konami 1994		
	Populous Acclaim 1991		
	Populous 2 - Trials of the Olympian Gods Imagineer 1993		
	Porky Pig´s Haunted Holiday Acclaim 1995		
	Power Drive U.S.Gold 1995		
	Power Piggs of the Dark Age Titus 1996		

Modul	Name	Inlay	OVP
	Power Rangers Bandai 1994		
	Power Rangers Zeo Battle Racers Bandai 1996		
	Power Monger Imagineer 1993		
	Prehistorik Man Titus 1996		
	Primal Rage Time Warner Interactive 1995		
	Prince of Persia Konami 1992		
	Prince of Persia 2 Titus 1996		
	Push over Featuring Giant Ocean 1992		
	Putty Squad Ocean 1994		
	Puzzle Bobble Bust a Move Taito Corporation 1995		
	R Type 3 - The third Ligthning Jaleco 1994		
	Race Drivin THQ 1992		
	Radical Rex Activision 1994		
	Ranma 1/2 NCS 1993		
	Realm Titus Software 1996		
	Ren & Stimpy Show the Time Warp THQ 1994		
	Ren& Stimpy Show the Veediots! THQ 1993		
	Revolution X Acclaim 1995		

Modul	Name	Inlay	OVP
	Rise of the Robots Acclaim 1994		
	Rival Turf Jaleco 1992		
	Road Riot 4WD THQ 1992		
	Robocop 3 Ocean 1992		
	Robocop vs. The Terminator Virgin 1993		
	Rock´n´Roll Racing Interplay 1993		
	Run Saber Atlus 1993		
	S.O.S. Sink or swimm Titus 1996		
	Sailermoon Bandai 1994		
	Samurai Showdown Takara 1994		
	Saturday Night Slammasters Capcom 1994		
	Schlümpfe, Die Infogrames 1994		
	Schlümpfe, Die - Reisen um die Welt Infogrames 1994		
	Scooby Doo Mystery Acclaim 1995		
	Sea Quest DSV Malibu 1995		
	Secret of Evermore Square Soft 1995		
	Secret of Mana Square Soft 1993		
	Sensible Soccer European Champions Sony 1994		

SNES 61

Modul	Name	Inlay	OVP
	Shadowrun Data East 1993		
	Shanghai 2 - Dragons Eye Activison 1993		
	Shaq-Fu EA 1994		
	Side Pocket Data East 1993		
	Sim City Nintendo 1991		
	Sim City 2000 Black Pearl 1996		
	Simpsons, The - Barts Nightmare Acclaim 1992		
	Skyblazer Sony 1994		
	Smash Tennis Virgin 1994		
	Soccer Kid Ocean 1994		
	Soccer Shootout Capcom 1994		
	Sonic Blast Man Taito 1993		
	Soul Blazer Enix America Inc. 1992		
	Space Ace Absolute Entertainment 1994		
	Space Invaders Nintendo 1997		
	Spanky´s Quest Natsume 1992		
	Sparkster Konami 1994		
	Spawn Acclaim 1995		

Modul	Name	Inlay	OVP
	Spectre Cybersoft 1994		
	Spider-Man LJN 1995		
	Spider Man - Venom - Maximum Carnage LJN 1994		
	Spider Man - X-Men - Arcade's Revenge LJN 1992		
	Sindizzy Worlds Activision 1993		
	Spirou Infogrames 1996		
	Star Trek - The Next Generation - Future's Past Spectrum Holobyte 1994		
	Star Trek - Deep Space Nine - Crossroads of Time Playmates 1995		
	Star Trek - Starfleet Academy Interplay 1994		
	Stargate Acclaim 1995		
	Starwing Nintendo 1993		
	Streetfighter Alpha 2 Capcom 1996		
	Streetfighter 2 - World Warrior Capcom 1992		
	Streetfighter 2 - Turbo Capcom 1993		
	Street Racer Ubisoft 1994		
	Striker Atlus 1993		
	Stunt Race FX Nintendo 1994		

Modul	Name	Inlay	OVP
	Sunset Riders Konami 1993		
	Super Adventures Island Hudson 1992		
	Super Adventures Island 2 Huson 1994		
	Super Air Driver Vic Tokai 1993		
	Super Aleste Toho 1992		
	Super B.C. Kid Hudson 1994		
	Supper Battleship Classic Naval Combat Game Mindscape 1993		
	Super Battletank 2 Absolute Entertainment 1994		
	Super Chase HQ Taito 1993		
	Super Conflict Vic Tokai 1993		
	Super Dany Virgin 1994		
	Super Double Dragon Tradewest 1992		
	Super Ghouls´n´Ghosts Capcom 1991		
	Super Goal! Jaleco 1992		
	Super Hockey Nintendo 1993		
	Super Ice Hockey Sunsoft 1994		
	Super International Cricket Nintendo 1994		
	Super James Pond Ocean 1993		

Modul	Name	Inlay	OVP
	Super Mario Allstars Nintendo 1993		
	Super Mario Kart Nintendo 1992		
	Super Mario RPG - Legend of the seven Seas Nintendo 1996		
	Super Mario World Nintendo 1991		
	Super Mario World 2 - Yoshi´s Island Nintendo 1995		
	Super Metroid Nintendo 1994		
	Super Morph Sony 1993		
	Super NES Scope 6 (mit Pistole) Nintendo 1992		
	Super Off Road Tradewest 1991		
	Super Pang Capcom 1992		
	Super Pinball behind the Mask Nintendo 1994		
	Super Probotector Alien Rebels Konami 1992		
	Super Punch Out ! Nintendo 1994		
	super Putty U.S. Gold 1993		
	Super R-Type Irem 1991		
	Super Smash T.V. Acclaim 1992		
	Super Soccer Nintendo 1992		
	Super Star Wars JVC 1992		

Modul	Name	Inlay	OVP
	Super Star Wars - Return of the Jedi JVC 1994		
	Super Star Wars - The Empire strikes back JVC 1993		
	Super Streetfighter 2 - The new Challengers Capcom 1994		
	Super Strike Eagle MicroProse 1993		
	Super Strike Gunner Activision 1992		
	Super Swiv Sunsoft 1992		
	Super Tennis Nintendo 1991		
	Super Troll Island Kemco 1994		
	Super Turrican Hudson Soft 1993		
	Super Turrican 2 Ocean 1995		
	Super Widget Atlus 1993		
	Syndicate Ocean 1995		
	Syvalion JVC 1993		
	T2 - The Arcade Game Acclaim 1994		
	Terminator, The Mindscape 1993		
	Terminator 2 - Judgement Day LJN 1993		
	Taz Mania Sunsoft 1993		
	Tecmo Super NBA Basketball Tecmo 1993		

Modul	Name	Inlay	OVP
	Teena ge Mutant Ninja Turtels - Tournament Fighters Konami 1993		
	Teena ge Mutant Ninja Turtels 4 - Turtles in Time Konami 1992		
	Terranigma Enix America Inc. 1996		
	Test Drive 2 - The Duel Ballistic 1992		
	Tetris 2 Nintendo 1994		
	Tetris Attack Nintendo 1996		
	Tetris & Dr. Mario Nintendo 1994		
	The Firemen Human Entertainment 1994		
	The Flinstones - Treasure of Sierra Madrock Taito 1994		
	The Humans Gametek 1993		
	The Hunt for Red October Hi-Tech 1993		
	The Incredible Hulk U.S.Gold 1994		
	The Itchy & Scratchy Game Acclaim 1995		
	The Legend of Mystical Ninja Konami 1992		
	The Legend of Zelda - A Link to the Past Nintendo 1992		
	Theme Park Ocean 1996		
	Thomas the Tank Engine & Friends THQ 1993		

Modul	Name	Inlay	OVP
	Tim in Tibet Infogrames 1995		
	Tim und der Sonnentempel Infogrames 1997		
	Time Trax Malibu Games 1994		
	Timecop JVC 1995		
	Timeslip Vic Tokai 1993		
	Tiny Toon Adventures Buster Busts Loose Konami 1993		
	Tiny Toon Adventures Wacky Sports Challenge Konami 1996		
	TKO Super Championship Boxing Sofel 1992		
	Tom and Jerry Hi-Tech 1993		
	Top Gear Kemco 1992		
	Top Gear 2 Kemco 1993		
	Top Gear 3000 Kemco 1995		
	Total Carnage Malibu 1993		
	Toys - lct thc Toy Wars Bcgin Absolute Entertainment 1993		
	Troddlers Seika Corp. 1993		
	Troy Aikmann NFL Football Tradewest 1994		
	True Lies LJN 1995		
	Tuff E Nuff Jaleco 1993		

Modul	Name	Inlay	OVP
	Turbo Toons Empire Interactive 1994		
	Turn and Burn - No Fly Zone Absolute Entertainment 1994		
	U.N. Squadron Capcom 1991		
	Ultimate Mortal Kombat 3 Williams 1996		
	Ultraman Bandai 1991		
	Unirally Nintendo 1994		
	Urban Strike - The Sequel to Jungle Strike Black Pearl 1995		
	Utopia - The Creation of a Nation Jaleco 1993		
	Val´d Isere Championship Mindscape 1994		
	Vegas Stakes Nintendo 1993		
	Venom / Spider-Man - Separation Anxiety Acclaim 1995		
	Virtual Bart Acclaim 1994		
	Virtual Soccer Hudson Soft 1994		
	Vortex Electro Brain 1994		
	Wario´s Woods Nintendo 1994		
	Warlock LJN 1994		
	Warp Speed Accolade 1992		
	Waterworld Ocean 1995		

SNES 69

Modul	Name	Inlay	OVP
	Wayne´s World THQ 1993		
	We´re Back - A Dinosaur Story HiTech 1993		
	Weapon Lord Namco 1995		
	Where in the World is Carmen Sandiego HiTech 1993		
	Whirlo Namco 1992		
	Whizz Titus Software 1996		
	Wild Guns Titus Software 1995		
	Wing Commander Minddscape 1992		
	Wing Commander - The Secret Missions Mindscape 1993		
	Winter Gold Nintendo 1996		
	Winter Olympics U.S.Gold 1994		
	Wolfenstein 3D Imagineer 1994		
	Wolverine Adamantioum Rage LJN 1994		
	World Championship Racing (Mansell) GameTek 1993		
	World Class Rugby Misawa 1993		
	World Cup Striker GameTek 1994		
	World Cup USA 94 U.S. Gold 1994		
	World Heroes Sunsoft 1993		

Modul	Name	Inlay	OVP
	World League Basketball Nintendo 1992		
	World Masters Golf Competition Edition Virgin 1995		
	Worms Ocean 1996		
	WWF Raw LJN 1994		
	WWF Royal Rumble LJN 1993		
	WWF Super Wrestlemania LJN 1992		
	WWF Wrestlemania - The Arcade Game Acclaim 1995		
	X Zone Kemco 1992		
	X-Kaliber 2097 Activision 1994		
	X-Men Mutant Apocalypse Capcom 1994		
	Yogi Bear´s Cartoon Capers Cybersoft 1994		
	Yoshi´s Cookie Bullet Proof Software 1993		
	Yoshi´s Safari Nintendo 1993		
	Young Merlin Virgin 1994		
	Zero - The Kamikaze Squirrel Sunsoft 1994		
	Zombies Konami 1993		
	Zool - Ninja of the „Nth" Dimension GameTek 1994		
	Zoop Viacom New Media 1995		

N64 Nintendo 64 bit Konsole (c)

Technische Daten: 64 Bit Videospielkonsole
Auflösung: 768 x 576 Pixel
RAM: 4 MB - erweiterbar auf 8 MB
CPU: 62,5 MHz
Speichermedium: Modul (512 Mbit)
Verkaufszeitraum Europa: 1996 bis 2003
Verkaufte Einheiten: 33 Millionen weltweit

Zubehör:

- Controller Pak (Speicherkarte)
- Rumble Pack
- Expansion Pak
- Transfer Pak

Modul	Name	Inlay	OVP
	007 James Bond - Die Welt ist nicht genug Eurocom 2000		
	1080 Snowboarding Nintendo 1998		
	AeroFighters Assault Video System 1997		
	Aero Gauge Ascii 1997		
	Aidyn Chronicles - The First Mage THQ 2001		
	Air Boarder 64 Human Entertainment 1988		
	All Star Baseball 99 Acclaim 1998		
	All Star Baseball 2000 Acclaim 1999		
	All Star Baseball 2001 Acclaim 2000		
	All Star Tennis 99 Ubisoft 1999		
	Arcade´s Greatest Hits 1 Midway 2000		
	Armorines Acclaim 1999		
	Army Men - Sarge´s Heroes 3DO 1999		
	Automobili Lamborghini Titus Software 1997		
	Banjo-Kazooie Nintendo 1998		
	Banjo-Tooie Nintendo 2000		
	Bass Hunter 64 Gear Head 1999		
	Batman of the Future - Return of the Joker Ubisoft 20000		

Modul	Name	Inlay	OVP
	Battle Tanx - Global Assault 3DO 1999		
	Beetle Adventure Racing EA 1999		
	Bio F.R.E.A.K.S. Midway 1998		
	Blast Corps Nintendo 1997		
	Blues Brothers 2000 Titus 2000		
	Body Harvest Midway 1998		
	Bomberman 64 Nintendo 1997		
	Bomberman Hero Nintendo 1998		
	Buck Bumble Ubisoft 1998		
	Bug´s Life, A Activision 1999		
	Bust-A-Move 99 Acclaim 1999		
	Bust-A-Move 2 - Arcade Edition Taito 1998		
	Carmageddon 64 Titus 2000		
	Castlevania Konami 1999		
	Castlevania - Legacy of Darkness Konami 1999		
	Centre Court Tennis Big Ben 1998		
	Chameleon Twist Sunsoft 1997		
	Chameleon Twist 2 Sunsoft 1999		

Modul	Name	Inlay	OVP
	Charlie Blast´s Territory Kemco 1999		
	Chopper Attack Midway 1998		
	ClayFighter 63 1/3 Interplay 1997		
	Command & Conquer Nintendo 1999		
	Conker´s Bad Fur Day Nintendo 2001		
	Cruis´n USA Midway 1996		
	Cruis´n World Midway 1998		
	Cyber Tiger EA 2000		
	Daikatana Kemco 2000		
	Dark Rift Vic Tokai 1997		
	Destruction Derby 64 THQ 1999		
	Diddy Kong Racing Nintendo 1997		
	Donald Duck´s Quack Attack Ubisoft 2000		
	Disney´s Tarzan Activsion 2000		
	Donkey Kong 64 Nintendo 1999		
	Doom 64 Midway 1997		
	Dual Heroes Electro Brain 1998		
	Duck Dodgers Starring Daffy Duck Atari 2000		

Modul	Name	Inlay	OVP
	Duke Nukem 64 GT Interactive 1997		
	Duke Nukem - Zero Hour GT Interactive 1999		
	Earthworm Jim 3D Rockstar Games 1999		
	ECW Hardcore Revolution Acclaim 2000		
	Excitebike 64 Nintendo 2000		
	Extreme G Acclaim 1997		
	Extreme G 2 Acclaim 1998		
	F1 World Grand Prix Video System 1998		
	F1 World Grand Prix II Video System 2000		
	F-Zero X Nintendo 1998		
	F1 Pole Position 64 Ubisoft 1997		
	F1 Racing Championship Ubisoft 2000		
	FIFA 99 EA 1998		
	FIFA Road to World Cup 98 EA 1997		
	FIFA Soccer 64 EA 1997		
	Fighters Destiny Ocean 1998		
	Fighting Force 64 Crave Entertainment 1999		
	Flying Dragon Natsume 1998		

Modul	Name	Inlay	OVP
	Flying Dragon Natsume 1998		
	Forsaken 64 Iguana UK 1998		
	G.A.S.P!! Fighter's NEXTream Konami 1998		
	Gauntlet Legends Midway 1998		
	Gex 3 - Deep Cover Gecko Crave Entertainment 1998		
	Gex 64 Midway 1998		
	Golden Eye 007 Nintendo 1997		
	GT 64 - Championship Edition Ocean 1998		
	Hercules - The Legendary Journeys Titus 2000		
	HeXen GT Interactive 1997		
	Holy Magic Century Konami 1999		
	Hot Wheels Turbo Racing EA 1999		
	Hybrid Heaven Konami 1999		
	Hydro Thunder Midway 2000		
	Iggy's Reckin' Balls Acclaim 1998		
	In-Fisherman Bass Hunter 64 Take 2 Interactive 1999		
	International Superstar Soccer 98 Konami 1998		
	Internation Superstar Soccer 2000 Konami 1999		

Modul	Name	Inlay	OVP
	Internation Superstar Soccer 64 Konami 1996		
	Internation Track & Field - Summer Games Konami 2000		
	Jeremy McGrath Supercross 2000 Acclaim 2000		
	Jet Force Gemini Nintendo 1999		
	Killer Instinct Gold Nintendo 1996		
	Kirby 64 - The Crystal Shards Nintendo 2000		
	Knife Edghe Kemco 1998		
	Knockout Kings 2000 EA 1999		
	Kobe Bryant in NBA Courtside Nintendo 1998		
	Legend of Zelda, The - Majora´s Mask Nintendo 2000		
	Legend of Zelda, The - Ocarina of Time Nintendo 1998		
	LEGO Racers Lego Media 1999		
	Lode Runner 3-D Infogrames 1999		
	Lylat Wars Nintendo 1997		
	Mace: The Dark Age Midway 1997		
	Madden 64 EA 1997		
	Madden NFL ´99 EA 1999		
	Magical Tetris Challenge Capcom 1999		

Modul	Name	Inlay	OVP
	Mario Golf Nintendo 1999		
	Mario Kart 64 Nintendo 1996		
	Mario Party Nintendo 1998		
	Mario Party 2 Nintendo 1999		
	Mario Party 3 Nintendo 2000		
	Mario Tennis Nintendo 2000		
	Michael Owen´s WLS 2000 THQ 2000		
	Mickey´s Speedway USA Nintendo 2000		
	Micro Machines 64 Turbo Midway 1999		
	Mischief Makers Nintendo 1997		
	Mission: Impossible Ocean 1998		
	Monaco Grand Prix Ubisoft 1999		
	Monster Truck Madness 64 Rockstar Games 1999		
	Mortal Kombat 4 Midway 1998		
	Mortal Kombat Mythologies - Sub Zero Midway 1997		
	Mortal Kombat Trilogy Midway 1996		
	Multi-Racing Championship Ocean 1997		
	Mystical Ninja - Starrin Goemon Konami 1997		

Modul	Name	Inlay	OVP
	Nagano Winter Olympics 98 Konami 1997		
	NASCAR 99 EA 1998		
	NBA Hangtime Midway 1997		
	NBA Pro 98 Konami 1998		
	NBA Pro 99 Konami 1999		
	NBA in the Zone 2000 Konami 2000		
	NBA Jam 99 Acclaim 1998		
	NBA Jam 2000 Acclaim 1999		
	NBA Live 99 EA 1998		
	NBA Live 2000 EA 1999		
	The New Tetris Nintendo 1999		
	NFL Quarterback Club 98 Acclaim 1997		
	NFL Quarterback Club 99 Acclaim 1998		
	NFL Quarterback Club 2000 Acclaim 1999		
	NHL 99 EA 1998		
	NHL Breakaway 99 Acclaim 1998		
	NHL Pro 99 Konami 1999		
	Nuclear Strike 64 THQ 1999		

Modul	Name	Inlay	OVP
	Off Road Challenge Midway 1998		
	Olympic Hockey Nagano 98 Midway 1998		
	Paper Mario Nintendo 2000		
	Paperboy 64 Midway 1999		
	Penny Racers THQ 1999		
	Perfect Dark Nintendo 2000		
	PGA European Tour Infogrames 2000		
	Pilotwings 64 Nintendo 1996		
	Pokemon Puzzle League Nintendo 2000		
	Pokemon Snap Nintendo 1999		
	Pokemon Stadium Nintendo 1999		
	Pokemon Stadium 2 Nintendo 2000		
	Power Rangers Lightspeed Rescue THQ 2000		
	Quake 64 Midway 1998		
	Quake II Activision 1999		
	Rainbow Six Red Storm Entertainment 1999		
	Rakuaga Kids Konami 1998		
	Rampage 2 - Universal Tour Midway 1999		

Modul	Name	Inlay	OVP
	Rampage World Tour Midway 1998		
	Rat Attack ! Mindscape 2000		
	Rayman 2 - The Great Escape Ubisoft 1999		
	Re-Volt Acclaim 1999		
	Ready 2 - Rumble Boxing Midway 1999		
	Resident Evil 2 Capcom 1999		
	Ridge Racer 64 Nintendo 2000		
	Road Rash 64 THQ 1999		
	Roadsters Titus Software 1999		
	Robotron 64 Crave Entertainment 1998		
	Rocket Robot on Wheels Ubisoft 1999		
	Rugrats in Paris - The Movie THQ 2000		
	Rugrats - Treasur Hunt THQ 1999		
	Rush 2 - Extreme Racing USA Midway 1998		
	S.C.A.R.S Ubisoft 1998		
	San Francisco Rush Midway 1997		
	San Francisco Rush 2049 Midway 2000		
	Scooby Doo! Classic Creep Capers THQ 2000		

Modul	Name	Inlay	OVP
	Shadow Man Acclaim 1999		
	Shadowgate 64 - Trials of the four Towers Kemco 1999		
	Snowboard Kids Atlus 1997		
	South Park Acclaim 1998		
	South Park Rally Acclaim 2000		
	South Park - Chef's Luv Shack Acclaim 1999		
	Space Station Silicon Valley Take 2 Interactive 1998		
	Star Wars - Episode I - Battle for Naboo Lucas Arts 2000		
	Star Wars - Episode I Racer Nintendo 1999		
	Star Wars - Roque Squadron Lucas Arts 1998		
	Star Wars - Shadows of the Empire Nintendo 1996		
	Starhot - Space Circus Fever Infogrames 1999		
	Super Mario 64 Nintendo 1996		
	Super Smash Bros. Nintendo 1999		
	Supercross 2000 EA 1999		
	Superman 64 Titus Software 1999		
	Taz Express Infogrames 2000		
	Tetrisphere Nintendo 1997		

Modul	Name	Inlay	OVP
	Tom & Jerry in Fist of Fury NewKidCo 2000		
	Tonic Trouble Ubisoft 1999		
	Tony Hawk's Skateboarding Activision 2000		
	Tony Hawk's Pro Skater Activision 2001		
	Top Gear Hyper Bike Kemco 2000		
	Top Gear Overdrive Kemco 1998		
	Top Gear Rally Midway 1997		
	Top Gear Rally 2 Kemco 1999		
	Toy Story 2 - Buzz Lightyear to the Rescue Activision 1999		
	Turok - Dinosaur Hunter Acclaim 1997		
	Turok 2 - Seeds of Evil Acclaim 1998		
	Turok 3 - Shadows of Oblivion 2000 Acclaim 2000		
	Turok - Rage Wars Acclaim 1999		
	Twisted Edge Snowboarding Midway 1998		
	V-Rally Edition 99 Infogrames 1999		
	Vigilante 8 Activision 1998		
	Vigilante 8 - Second Offense Activision 1999		
	Virtual Chess 64 Titus Software 1998		

Modul	Name	Inlay	OVP
	Virtual Pool 64 Crave Entertainment 1998		
	Waialae Country Club - True Golf Classics Nintendo 1997		
	War Gods Midway 1997		
	Wave Race Nintendo 1996		
	Wayne Gretzky´s 3D Hockey Midway 1996		
	WCW Mayhem EA 1999		
	WCW vs nWo - World Tour THQ 1997		
	WCW / nWo - Revenge THQ 1998		
	Wetrix Ocean 1998		
	WinBack Koei 1999		
	Winnie the Pooh - Tiggers Honey Hunt NewKidCo 2000		
	Wipeout 64 Midway 1998		
	World Cup 98 EA 1998		
	World Driver Championship Midway 1999		
	Worms Armageddon Infogrames 2000		
	WWF Attitude Acclaim 1999		
	WWF No Mercy THQ 2000		
	WWF War Zone Acclaim 1998		

Modul	Name	Inlay	OVP
	WWF WrestleMania 2000 THQ 1999		
	Xena - Warrior Princess - The Talisman of Fate Titus Software 1999		
	Yoshi´s Story Nintendo 1997		

Herstellung und Verlag:
BoD - Books on Demand, Norderstedt
ISBN 978-3-8370-9171-7